100%

GET THE WHOLE PICTURE

PEOPLE AND PLACES

PAUL MASON

Cavendish Square

Published in 2024 by Cavendish Square Publishing, LLC
2544 Clinton Street, Buffalo, NY 14224

First published in Great Britain in 2020 by Wayland

Website: cavendishsq.com

Series editor: Elise Short
Produced by Tall Tree Ltd
Editor: Lara Murphy
Designer: Jonathan Vipond

Picture Credits
t-top, b-bottom, l-left, r-right, c-center, front cover-fc, back cover-bc
Shutterstock: 1bl, 9br Djent, 1br, 19tl ESB Professional, 1tr, 5bl Thamyris Salgueiro, 5bl Sophie James, 6b Luciano Mortula – LGM, 10-11t Zhukova Valentyna, 10bl Dan Breckwoldt, 11r Donna Beeler, 15t ymgerman, 17bl cowardlion, 17bcr Mia2you, 17br f11photo, 19tr Diego Grandi, 19br Robert Szymanski, 20tl Vector Tradition, 21b Yongyut Kumsri, 23b nenets, 23tr Shchipkova Elena, 24-25t MrLis, 24br Adwo, 25tr Emily Marie Wilson, 25b sljones, 26t Adwo, 26br Volodymyr Burdiak, 27b Melissa Schalke, 27tr Tyler Olson, 28lt karnoff, 29tr vectorsicon.com, Creative Commons: 15cr USGS EROS Data Center, 18bl Omegatron, 28-29 NASA/Crew of STS-132, 29b NASA

Cataloging-in-Publication Data

Names: Mason, Paul.
Title: People and places / Paul Mason.
Description: Buffalo, New York : Cavendish Square Publishing, 2024. | Series: 100% get the whole picture | Includes glossary and index.
Identifiers: ISBN 9781502668752 (pbk.) | ISBN 9781502668769 (library bound) | ISBN 9781502668776 (ebook)
Subjects: LCSH: Human geography--Juvenile literature. | Dwellings--Juvenile literature. | Manners and customs--Juvenile literature.
Classification: LCC GF48.M376 2024 | DDC 304.2--dc23

CPSIA compliance information: Batch #CSCSQ24: For further information contact Cavendish Square Publishing LLC at 1-877-980-4450.

Printed in the United States of America

CONTENTS

All measurements in this book are presented in metric, as they are the units most scientists prefer to work in.

People and places

How people live—what their home is like, the job they do, the clothes they wear and more—is affected by the place they live in.

Someone who lives by the sea, for example, is much more likely to be a fisherman than a person who lives in a desert.

20%

OF PEOPLE LIVE INLAND

80%

OF PEOPLE LIVE WITHIN 100 KM OF THE COAST

7,595,978,197 NUMBER OF PEOPLE ON EARTH WHEN THIS BOOK WAS BEING WRITTEN

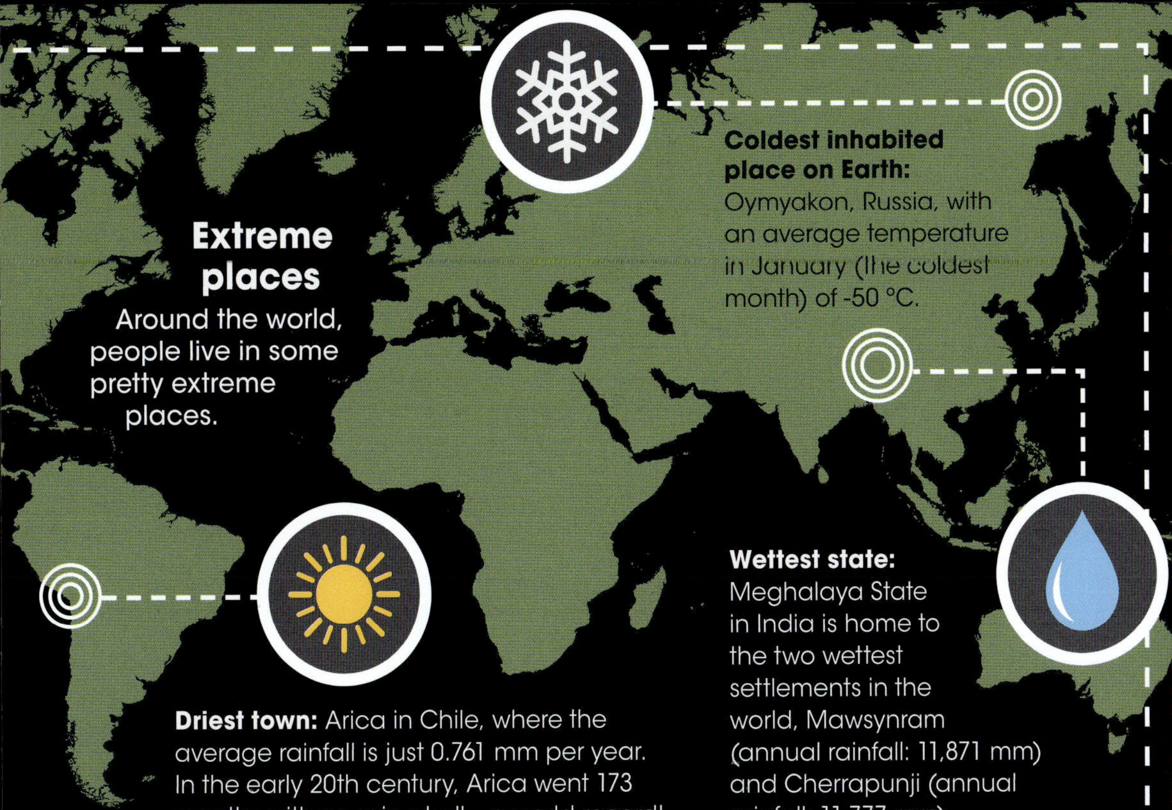

Extreme places

Around the world, people live in some pretty extreme places.

Coldest inhabited place on Earth: Oymyakon, Russia, with an average temperature in January (the coldest month) of -50 °C.

Driest town: Arica in Chile, where the average rainfall is just 0.761 mm per year. In the early 20th century, Arica went 173 months with no rain at all—a world record!

Wettest state: Meghalaya State in India is home to the two wettest settlements in the world, Mawsynram (annual rainfall: 11,871 mm) and Cherrapunji (annual rainfall: 11,777 mm).

Location is everything

Of course, not everyone lives in such an extreme location. In fact, most humans now live in cities. Even there, though, the environment affects how they live.

Winnipeg

In cold, snowy Winnipeg, Canada, the average temperature in winter is about -16°C, so you need a warm home and plenty of clothes.

Kuwait City

Meanwhile in Kuwait City, the capital of Kuwait, the average temperature in summer is around 41°C. People wear loose, thin clothes and most buildings are air-conditioned.

In fact, in the time it took to write these sentences, the world's population went up to **7,595,978,253.** These people all need to live somewhere.

Cities or countryside?

In 2016, 54 percent of the world's people lived in cities. People often move to cities looking for job opportunities and a better standard of living.

Spread of cities

In cities, lots of people live close together. Many cities first formed at trading locations, such as next to natural harbors or on rivers. Over time, the original cities have spread out, becoming large urban areas.

By 2050, the United Nations predicts that:

68%

OF THE WORLD'S POPULATION WILL BE URBAN

Tokyo, Japan

Megacities

A megacity is one that has 10,000,000 or more people living in it.

- In 1975 there were only three megacities: Tokyo, New York and Mexico City.
- By 2000, this number had grown to 16 megacities.
- The United Nations predicts that by 2030 there will be 43 megacities.

Already more than 75 percent of people in Australia, Brazil, Japan, the UK, and the U.S. (among many other countries) live in cities.

38,000,000

THE NUMBER OF PEOPLE THOUGHT TO LIVE IN GREATER TOKYO, THE WORLD'S LARGEST MEGACITY, IN 2016

That's the same as the number of the **global** population in the year 3564 BCE.

What is rural?

In rural areas, there are fewer people, and they are more widely spread out than in a city. Farming is often an important industry. Trees, plants and wild animals are more widespread.

rural landscape in Thailand

32%

OF THE WORLD'S POPULATION WILL BE RURAL

Tropical rain forests

25%
OF ALL THE WORLD'S INSECT SPECIES ARE THOUGHT TO LIVE IN THE RAIN FOREST CANOPY

Tropical rain forests grow near the equator. They have a lot of rainfall and high temperatures all year round.

Indigenous people

People have been living in tropical rain forests for thousands of years. The hot, wet climate makes these forests very fertile, so food is plentiful.

The original inhabitants of a place are known as "indigenous."

- 500 years ago, the giant Amazon rain forest may have been home to 10,000,000 indigenous people.
- Today there are about 1,000,000.
- Most were killed by diseases brought by people from outside the Amazon.

blue morpho butterfly, Peru, South America

palm oil plantation, east Asia

Settlers

Increasing numbers of settlers are moving to rain forests. Many move there to farm. Others work at palm oil plantations, or in the logging or gold mining industries.

7,000,000 km²

SIZE OF THE AMAZON RIVER BASIN, HOME TO THE WORLD'S BIGGEST RAIN FOREST

If the Amazon basin was a country, it would be the world's seventh largest.

Disappearing forests

Tropical rain forests are being cut down more quickly than new trees can grow. Satellite images show that:

- in the 1990s, 404,000 km^2 were cut down
- in the 2000s, 654,000 km^2 were cut down

Why are tropical rain forests being cut down?

40% FOR SMALL FARMS

22.5% FOR CATTLE FARMS

17.5% FOR LARGE FARMS

12.5% FOR LOGGING

7.5% FOR OTHER REASONS*

*These include housebuilding, new roads, forest fires, hydroelectric plants and fuelwood.

80% OF THE WORLD'S PLANT FOODS ARE THOUGHT TO HAVE ORIGINATED FROM TROPICAL RAIN FORESTS, INCLUDING BANANAS, COFFEE AND COCOA

Temperate rain forests

Temperate rain forests are cool and wet. Many have an average temperature of 4–12 °C and receive up to 1,500 mm of rainfall each year.

Human settlements

Humans have lived in temperate rain forests for tens of thousands of years.

The combination of high rainfall, rivers, a mild climate and wildlife makes the forests rich in food, such as fruits and nuts.

Temperate rain forests are found mostly in cooler parts of the world, close to coasts.

The Pacific Northwest

The indigenous peoples of the Pacific Northwest include the Haida, Tlingit, Chinook and Coast Salish.

In the past, salmon from the region's rivers was their most important food. The people carved huge sea-going canoes and totem poles (below) from giant forest trees.

35%

OF TEMPERATE RAIN FOREST IS IN THE PACIFIC NORTHWEST OF NORTH AMERICA

Potlatch

In the Pacific Northwest, some indigenous people had a custom called potlatch. This custom relied on the plentiful food and resources of the rain forest.

It involved having a huge feast, then giving away generous gifts. Potlatch was banned for many years by the U.S. and Canadian governments. After the ban was lifted, some communities started practicing this custom again.

giant trees grow in temperate rain forests

10,000 mm

AMOUNT OF RAIN THAT FALLS EACH YEAR ON THE TEMPERATE RAIN FORESTS OF YAKUSHIMA ISLAND, JAPAN

Much like the tropical rain forests, the temperate rain forests are threatened by extreme weather caused by climate change and by deforestation caused by logging.

loggers working in a North American forest in the 1800s

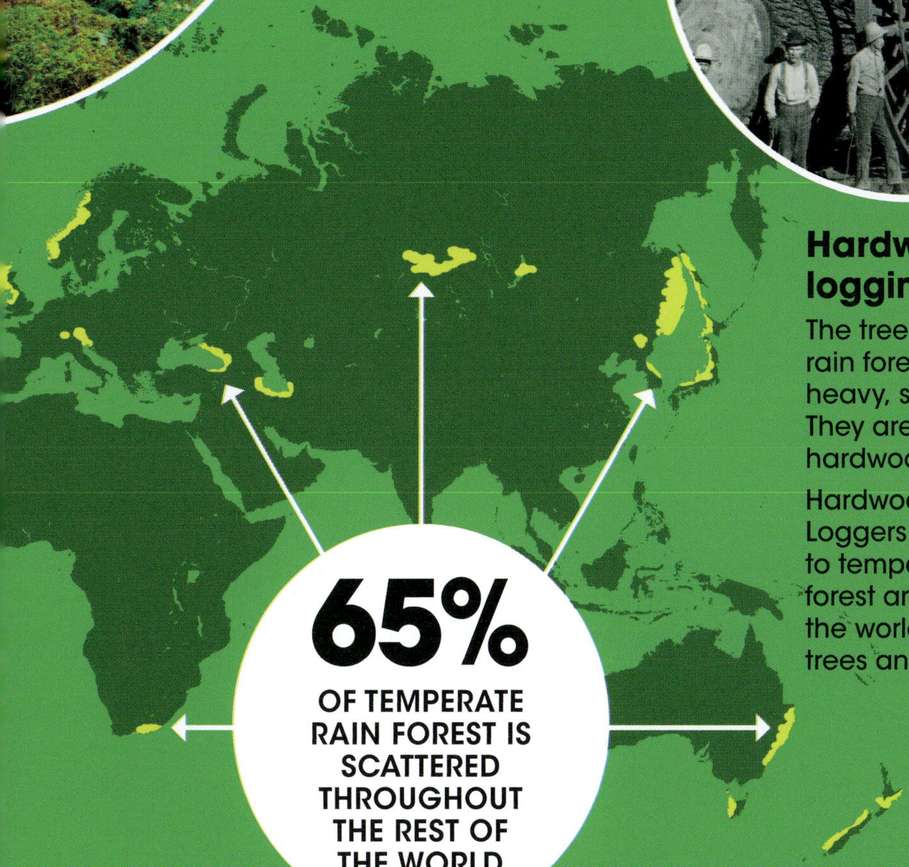

Hardwood logging

The trees in temperate rain forests have heavy, strong wood. They are called hardwood trees.

Hardwood is valuable. Loggers have moved to temperate rain forest areas around the world to cut down trees and sell them.

65%

OF TEMPERATE RAIN FOREST IS SCATTERED THROUGHOUT THE REST OF THE WORLD

Mountains

A mountain is a very big hill with steep slopes. There is no agreed rule about exactly how high a mountain is, but most are over 600 meters tall.

sherpa in the Himalayan mountains

Relatively few people live at these high altitudes.

10%
OF THE WORLD'S PEOPLE LIVE IN MOUNTAIN REGIONS

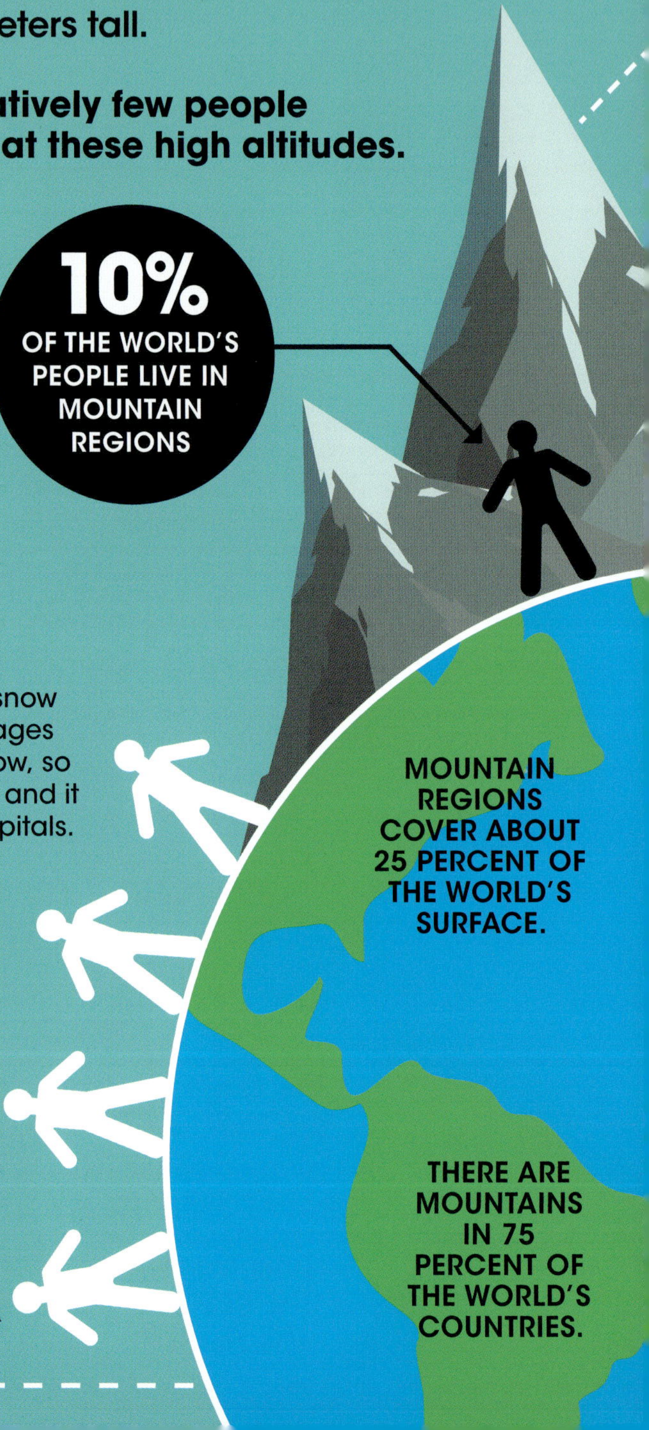

Mountain living

Life in the mountains can be tough. Travel can be hard work; in winter, snow sometimes traps people in their villages for weeks on end. Food may not grow, so people have to rely on stored food, and it is difficult to get to schools and hospitals.

14,232,088

POPULATION OF THE EUROPEAN ALPS, THE WORLD'S MOST POPULATED MOUNTAIN REGION, IN 2012. THIS EQUALS 74.6 PEOPLE PER KM².

That same year, Paris, the most tightly packed city in Europe, had 21,616 people per km². That's almost 300 times as many.

skier in the French Alps

Tourism

Millions of tourists visit mountainous regions each year.

- In summer, hiking and cycling are the most popular activities.
- In winter, people come for the skiing, snowboarding and snowshoeing.

Long-distance talking

In some mountain areas, people have developed their own "languages," or ways of passing simple messages from mountain to mountain.

In Turkey, people in the Pontic Mountains use a kind of whistle-talking.

Switzerland is famous for its yodelers.

Himalayan mountains, Nepal

90%

OF PEOPLE LIVE OUTSIDE MOUNTAIN REGIONS

The Death Zone

In the Himalayan and Karakoram mountains, there are 14 peaks with a "Death Zone."

These Death Zones are over 8,000 m high. There is so little oxygen that humans cannot survive in them for long.

Lakes and rivers

We all need fresh water to survive. Most human settlements developed close to a lake or river.

Far from water

Even today, when people can have water piped to their homes from far away, most of us still live close to a lake or river.

50% OF PEOPLE LIVE WITHIN 3 KM OF A LAKE OR RIVER

40% OF PEOPLE ARE 3–10 KM AWAY

10% OF PEOPLE ARE OVER 10 KM AWAY

Fishing for food

Around the world, rivers and lakes provide millions of people with fish and other food to eat.

In some places, such as Lake Victoria in Africa, too many fish have been caught and they have begun to run out.

fisherman on Lake Victoria

Overfishing

Nile perch is a popular catch in Lake Victoria. This fish can grow to more than 1.3 m long, but by 2017, over 90 percent were less than 50 cm long. Because people are catching them faster than they can grow, almost all the bigger fish have already been taken.

cargo ship on the Yangtze, China

River traders

Rivers are important trade routes.

The Yangtze, in China, is the world's busiest trade river, with over a billion tonnes of goods shipped along it per year.

This is twice as much as along the Mississippi River in the U.S. and five times as much as along the Rhine River in Germany.

90%

THE AMOUNT OF THE ARAL SEA, ONCE THE WORLD'S FOURTH-LARGEST LAKE, THAT HAS DISAPPEARED SINCE THE 1960S DUE TO WATER BEING DIVERTED FOR CROP IRRIGATION

82,100 km² **THE SIZE OF LAKE SUPERIOR IN NORTH AMERICA, THE LARGEST FRESHWATER LAKE IN THE WORLD BY AREA**

About **630,000** people live around Lake Superior.

Lake Baikal in Russia is the largest lake by volume at **23,013 km³**. It is **1,642 m deep.**

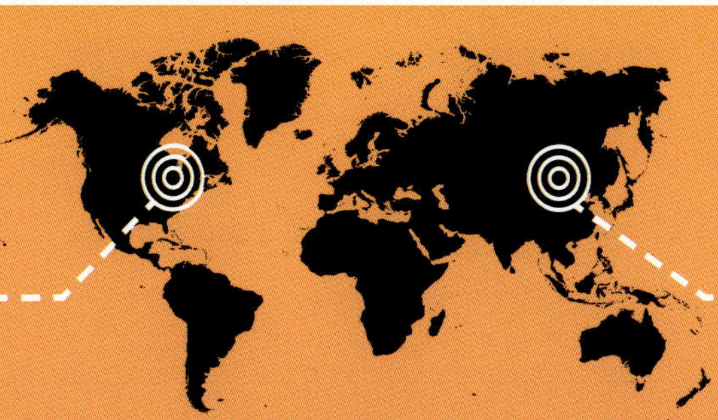

Coasts

In the past, life by the sea was mainly for fishermen and traders. Today, coastal living is popular with lots of people, due to the work opportunities, sports and tourism they offer.

Coastal population increases

The number of people living close to the sea is rising all the time.

In 2014, for example, 38 percent of Americans lived near the coast—even though coastal areas make up less than 10 percent of the U.S. More pople move to coastal areas every year.

Sea level rises

Our coasts are changing because of global warming. As ice caps melt and warmer water expands, sea levels are rising. By the year 2100, they will be approximately 2 m higher, which will flood many low-lying coastal areas.

Coastal building

On many coasts and estuaries, new houses, marinas, hotels and other facilities are being built. This affects the local animals and plants as coastal mangroves are destroyed.

Mangroves

Over 35 percent of the world's coastal mangrove forests have already been cut down.

- Sharks and other fish can no longer use the mangroves as nurseries.
- The mangrove roots no longer hold the coast together, making it vulnerable to erosion.

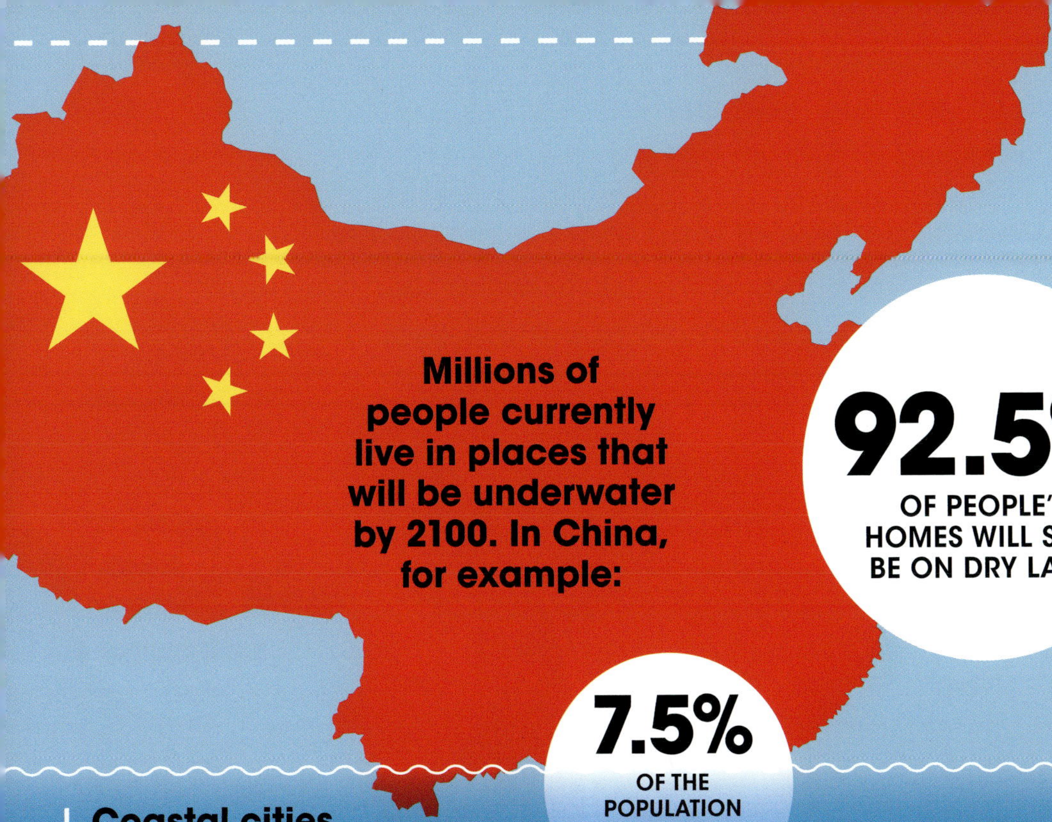

Millions of people currently live in places that will be underwater by 2100. In China, for example:

92.5%

OF PEOPLE'S HOMES WILL STILL BE ON DRY LAND

7.5%

OF THE POPULATION WILL BE FLOODED OUT*

Coastal cities

Many of the world's major cities are on the coast. As sea levels rise, millions of people living in coastal cities will be affected.

*7.5 percent may not sound like much—but in China, it would be over **82 million** people!

17,500,000

NUMBER OF PEOPLE IN SHANGHAI, CHINA, LIKELY TO BE AFFECTED BY SEA LEVEL RISES BY THE YEAR 2100

5,200,000 will be affected by flooding in Osaka, Japan

3,000,000 in Alexandria, Egypt

2,700,000 in Miami, U.S.

1,800,000 in Rio de Janeiro, Brazil

Islands

An island is a piece of land that is completely surrounded by water. Some islands are found in rivers and lakes, but most are in the sea.

What makes an island an island?

There is no set definition. In 1861, the British government said an island was a piece of land either:

(a) big enough to live on, or

(b) with enough summer grass for at least one sheep.

Just Enough Room Island, USA

Island size

Islands range in size from tiny to huge.

- A child could throw a stone across the world's smallest inhabited island, Just Enough Room Island in New York State, which covers just over 300 square meters.
- It takes about 25 days to ski-tour across the southern part of Greenland, the world's biggest island, which covers nearly 2.2 million square kilometers.

Hong Kong, China

Florianópolis, Brazil

96%

OF GREECE'S ISLANDS ARE UNINHABITED

Trade

Many of the world's most famous trading posts (settlements used for trading) began on islands. Today they have become major cities. Examples include Hong Kong (China) and Florianópolis (Brazil).

Global warming

Many islands sit just above sea level. As global warming causes sea levels to rise, they may be flooded.

Kiribati is a group of low-lying islands in the Pacific Ocean. In 2012, plans were made for the population of about 110,000 to move elsewhere when their country disappears beneath the waves. This could happen in the next 50 years.

flooding in Kiribati

Java, Indonesa

141,370,000

NUMBER OF PEOPLE LIVING ON JAVA, INDONESIA, IN 2015. JAVA IS THE WORLD'S MOST POPULATED ISLAND.

At least 15 other islands have populations of over 10 million.

The Arctic

The Arctic is a frozen region in Earth's far north. It is so cold and barren that few plants can grow there, and animals have to work hard to survive.

Harsh environment

Because there is so little vegetation, the Arctic's indigenous people traditionally lived off what they could hunt. Their diets mainly consisted of meat and fish.

The difficult conditions mean only a few people live in the Arctic. Although it is 9.7 percent of Earth's land surface:

99.47%
OF PEOPLE LIVE SOUTH OF THE ARCTIC

Arctic countries

Eight countries have Arctic territory: Canada, Finland, Greenland, Iceland, Norway, Russia, Sweden and the U.S.

0.53%
OF THE WORLD'S POPULATION LIVES IN THE ARCTIC

constant night to constant day

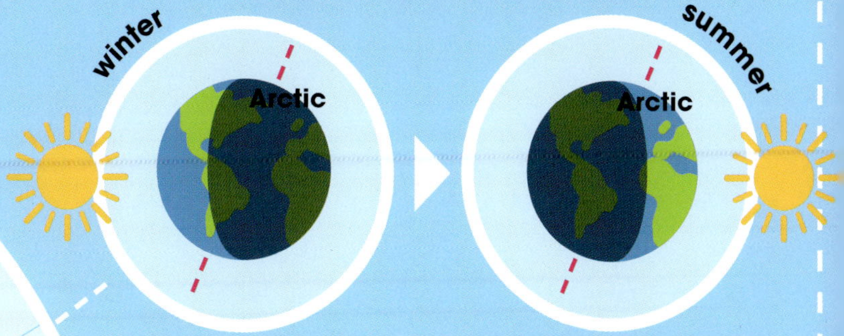

In winter, the Arctic region tilts away from the sun. It is dark for weeks on end.

In summer, Earth's north is tilted toward the sun.

It is light in the northern Arctic for 24 hours a day.

-68°C LOWEST TEMPERATURE EVER RECORDED IN THE ARCTIC

The temperature has gotten this cold twice, both times in Siberia, Russia: in 1885 at Verkhoyansk, and in 1933 at Oymyakon.

New settlers

In recent decades, new settlers have been moving to the Arctic, often to work in the mining or energy industries, or on military bases.

The settlers' warm, modern houses and food from the south are now popular with indigenous people too. The traditional Arctic hunting lifestyle is disappearing.

settlement in Kulusuk, East Greenland

Life on the tundra

The tundra is a zone of land south of the frozen Arctic and north of the milder forest zone. It covers 10 percent of Earth's land.

Frozen soil

About 1 m down, the tundra soil is permanently frozen. This is called permafrost. In the active layer of soil, above the permafrost, tough grass, moss and lichen grow.

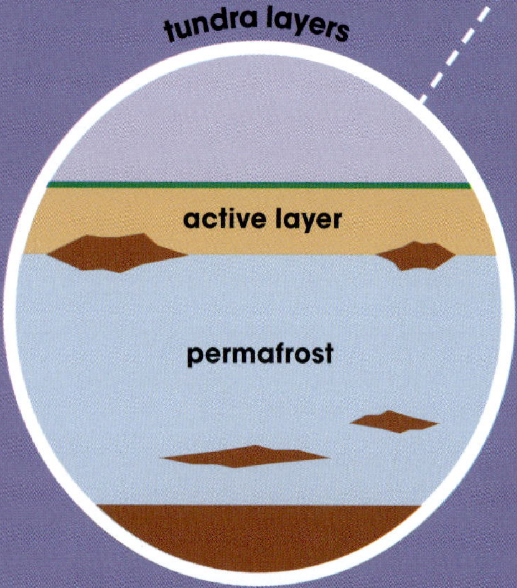

Global warming is changing the tundra.

If the Earth's temperature rises by 1.5°C:

25% OF THE PERMAFROST COULD MELT

75% MAY REMAIN FROZEN

Melting permafrost problems

- The greenhouse gases (carbon dioxide and methane) that were trapped in the ice are released.
- New plants and animals move into the environment, changing the ecosystem and forcing out plants and animals that had made it their home.
- Ancient bacteria and viruses may be released as the soil thaws.

Reindeer herders

The tundra's indigenous people are traditionally nomadic herders. They move with their herds to find food.

traditional Sámi reindeer herding, Finland

1,000 km

ROUGHLY HOW FAR REINDEER HERDERS FROM THE TUNDRA TRAVEL EACH YEAR WITH THEIR HERDS

North in summer

The herders move north during the summer. The warmer weather means there is food for their animals, and the winds keep biting insects away.

South in winter

As winter approaches, the herders pack up their tents. They move south of the tundra, to the shelter of the forest zone.

temporary homes of nomadic reindeer herders

Moving to towns

Some indigenous tundra people have now moved to towns, where they can live a more comfortable life. Others carry on with their traditional lifestyle.

Deserts

A desert is a place that receives less than 250 mm of precipitation each year. Roughly 30 percent of all land on Earth is desert.

The Sahara

The Sahara in North Africa is the world's second-biggest desert.

It has a population of up to 2.5 million people. Most live in cities at the edge of the desert.

Saharan sand dunes

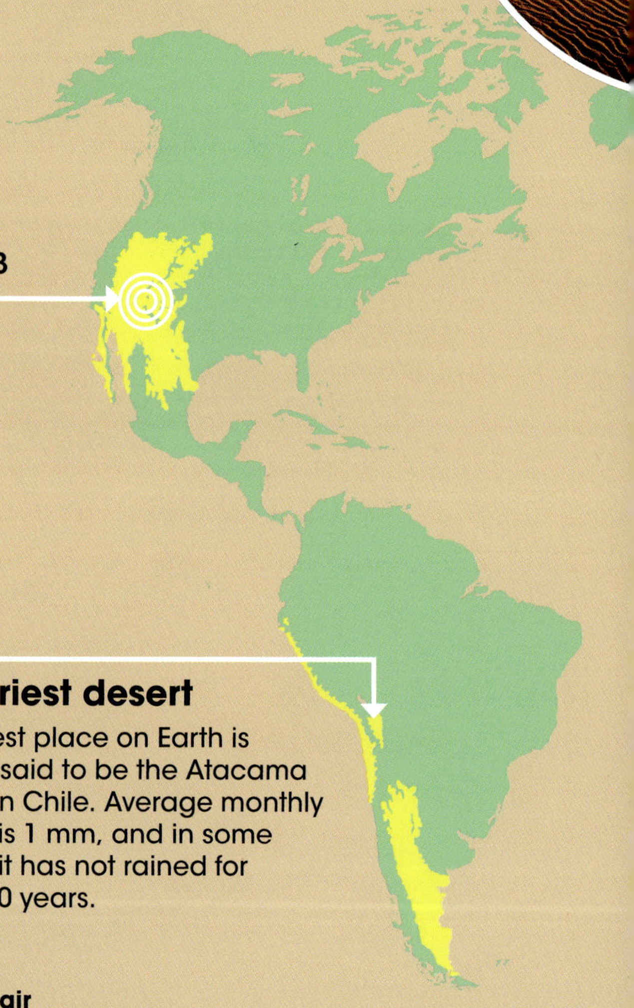

56.7 °C

TEMPERATURE RECORDED IN DEATH VALLEY, USA IN 1913

Death Valley is the hottest place on Earth, as well as the driest place in the U.S.

Atacama Desert, Chile

The driest desert

The driest place on Earth is usually said to be the Atacama Desert in Chile. Average monthly rainfall is 1 mm, and in some places it has not rained for over 400 years.

Water from the air

Today in the Atacama, water is harvested from the air.

Fine nets capture moisture from fog. Droplets then fall from the nets into large containers.

Saharan nomads

The Sahara has been home to nomadic people since 6000 BCE.

Today, descendants of these nomads still live in the Sahara Desert. They include the Tuareg people.

a Tuareg man leading desert camels

25%
OF SAHARAN PEOPLE ARE TUAREG

75%
ARE NON-TUAREG
FROM COUNTRIES INCLUDING ALGERIA, CHAD, EGYPT, LIBYA, MALI, MAURITANIA, MOROCCO, NIGER, SUDAN, TUNISIA AND WESTERN SAHARA

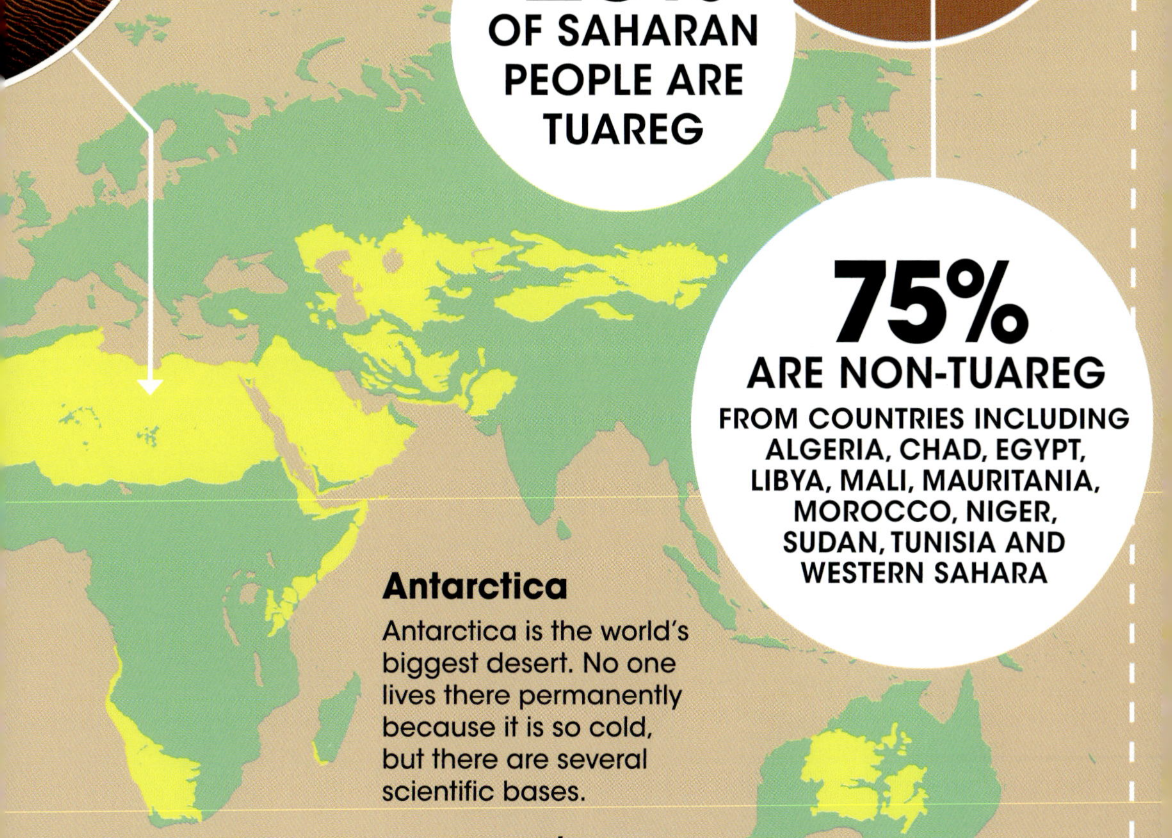

Antarctica

Antarctica is the world's biggest desert. No one lives there permanently because it is so cold, but there are several scientific bases.

scientists live and work in Antarctica

Grasslands

Grasslands are usually found between forest and desert zones. They grow where there is not enough rain for lots of trees, but too much rain for a desert.

cattle herders in Kenya

Grassland names

Grasslands have many names.

- **pampas** in South America
- **prairie** in North America
- **savanna** or **veldt** in Africa
- **steppe** in eastern Europe and Asia
- **rangelands** in Australia

Kilimanjaro National Park, Tanzania

People and grasslands

Grasslands are ideal for:

a) grazing animals, or hunting wild herds

b) growing crops.

Because of this, most grassland people were originally either nomadic herders, hunters or farmers.

Helpful horses

Horses are closely connected to grassland peoples. On horseback, it is easy to herd or hunt animals such as bison.

In North America, horses arrived with European settlers in the 17th century. Their use then spread among indigenous peoples.

Soon horses were being used to hunt huge herds of bison on the prairies.

Grassland is sometimes protected by law, so that it stays a wild place.

large farm, Central Asia

Grassland to farmland

Many wild grasslands have now been converted into farmland.

In Russia in the 1950s, for example, 430,000 km² of wild grassland was turned into farms. This was an area the same size as all of Canada's farmland.

8%

OF THE WORLD'S WILD GRASSLAND AND ITS WILDLIFE ARE PROTECTED

92%

IS UNPROTECTED AND COULD BE CHANGED FROM ITS WILD STATE

bison on North American grassland

29,001,000

ESTIMATED NUMBER OF BISON KILLED BY PEOPLE IN NORTH AMERICA BETWEEN 1820 AND 1880

This left roughly 1,000 bison living in the wild, bringing them close to extinction.

Space

Humans already live in some of the hottest, coldest, wettest and driest places on Earth. Some people think that the next place we move into could be space.

Air, water and food

Air, water and food are not found in space unless they are brought from Earth.

Fortunately, the machines aboard the International Space Station (ISS) are able to collect old water and clean it for reuse. They can also produce oxygen for astronauts to breathe.

The International Space Station

Humans have been living aboard the ISS since 2000. We now have lots of information about the challenges of living in space.

The ISS is the largest object ever built in space. It was put together over a number of years using modules and parts built by different countries, including the U.S., Russia, Canada, Japan and European countries.

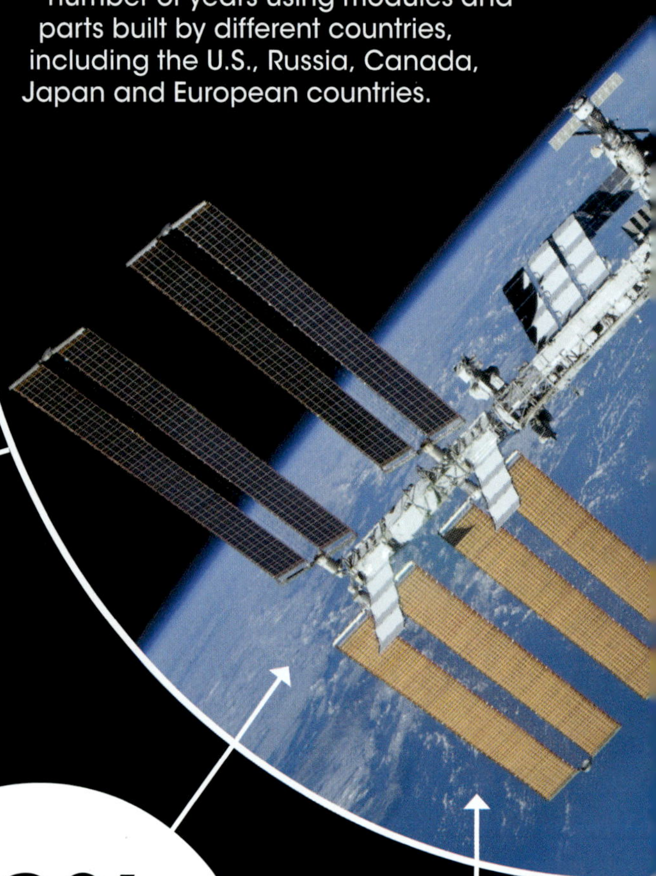

93% OF THE WATER USED ABOARD THE ISS IS RECLAIMED

7% IS BROUGHT TO THE ISS FROM EARTH

630,288 minutes

HOW LONG RUSSIAN COSMONAUT VALERI POLYAKOV SPENT IN SPACE (THE LONGEST TIME EVER)

That's **10,504 hours and 48 minutes** on board the Mir space station … or **437.7 days** … or **one year, two months, and twelve days**.

Sleeping

The ISS orbits Earth every 93 minutes, so there are sunrises and sunsets happening every 93 minutes as well. It's hard to know when you should be asleep. On the ISS, the astronauts usually sleep in darkened pods.

No gravity

Without Earth's gravity, there is no down or up.

Tasks such as putting salt on your food or going to the toilet on the ISS are very different from doing them on Earth!

Keeping fit

Human bodies are designed to work with Earth's gravity. Without it, things start to go wrong.

- Bones and muscles weaken.
- The heart and circulatory system become less efficient.
- Eyesight deteriorates.

In order to reduce these effects, astronauts aboard the ISS have to exercise regularly.

Glossary

bacteria
Tiny single-celled creatures. Some bacteria are responsible for diseases in humans, but other bacteria help keep us healthy.

barren
When relating to land, this means an area that is not able to grow plants.

bison
A humpbacked, shaggy type of wild ox that is found in North America and Europe.

convert
To change from one form into another.

equator
An imaginary line running around the middle of the Earth, where temperatures are high.

erosion
Wearing away; for example, soil erosion means that soil is being worn away, usually by wind or water.

estuary
The place where a river meets the sea and the water may sometimes be salty.

extinction
The complete destruction of a living thing.

fertile
When relating to land, this means able to grow plants.

global warming
The increase in Earth's average air and sea temperatures, which almost all scientists agree is linked to greenhouse gas emissions.

indigenous
Belonging to a particular place; for example, polar bears are indigenous to the Arctic.

logger
A person who cuts down trees.

nomadic
Moving to a new place with animals at set times of the year, in order to find them new food sources.

precipitation
Water from the air. Precipitation can be in the form of rain, snow, sleet, fog or mist.

river basin
An area of land that feeds water into a particular river.

terraced
When relating to farming, this means a series of fields that has been cut into a hillside.

trading post
A place where people gather to trade, sell or buy goods.

urban landscape
An area covered mostly with buildings, with few trees or plants and lots of people living close together.

virus
A tiny organism that can reproduce inside the cells of living things. Viruses cause many ailments, from the common cold to serious diseases.

volume
The amount of space an object takes up.

FURTHER INFORMATION

Books to read

The Lonely Planet Kids Travel Book: Mind-Blowing Stuff on Every Country in the World
(Lonely Planet Kids, 2015)
One for armchair travellers everywhere: as well as how people live in over 200 different countries, this book has information on animals, food, festivals and more.

People on Earth
Jon Richards and Ed Simkins (Wayland 2015)
Fun, colorful graphics delve into a massive range of subjects, from the origins of humans to the speed of urbanization and how countries are governed. Part of the Mapographica series.

The Manmade World
Jon Richards and Ed Simkins (Wayland 2015)
This book explores everything from skyscrapers to space missions. Part of the Mapographica series.

A World of Cities
James Brown and Lili Murray
(Walker Studio, 2017)
Explore 30 of the greatest cities in existence. From Paris to St. Petersburg, New York to Amsterdam and more, each page is beautifully illustrated and contains some surprising facts.

Places to visit

American Museum of Natural History
200 Central Park West
New York, NY 10024
Some of this museum's permanent exhibits include the history of indigenous peoples of the Pacific Northwest, a look at New York State's geography and the diversity of North America's forests.

Carnegie Museum of Natural History
4400 Forbes Avenue
Pittsburgh, PA 15213
Learn about dinosaurs, plants, ancient cultures and much more at this amazing museum.

National Museum of Natural HIstory
1000 Madison Drive NW
Washington, DC 20560
This museum, which is run by the Smithsonian Institute, has incredible exhibits about human history as well as the natural world.

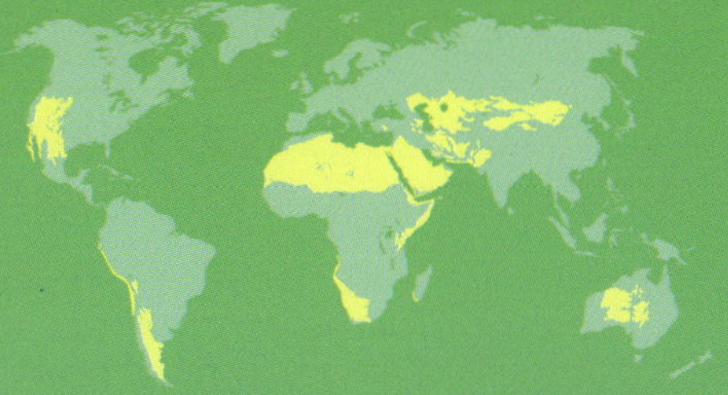

HOW TO READ BIG NUMBERS

1,000,000,000,000,000,000,000,000,000,000 = one nonillion
1,000,000,000,000,000,000,000,000,000 = one octillion
1,000,000,000,000,000,000,000,000 = one septillion
1,000,000,000,000,000,000,000 = one sextillion
1,000,000,000,000,000,000 = one quintillion
1,000,000,000,000,000 = one quadrillion
1,000,000,000,000 = one trillion
1,000,000,000 = one billion
1,000,000 = one million
1,000 = one thousand
100 = one hundred
10 = ten
1 = one

Index